Theory Paper Grade 4   1995   A

Duration 2 hours

Candidates should answer ALL questions.
Write your answers on this paper — no others will be accepted.
Answers must be written clearly and neatly — otherwise marks may be lost.

TOTAL MARKS
100

1 (a) Complete the time signature and add the missing bar-lines to the following.

10

Haydn, Keyboard Sonata, Hob.XVI/18

(b) Rewrite bars 1 and 2 in notes of *double the value*, and complete the time signature.

2 **EITHER**
   (a) Write a rhythm on one note, with time signature and bar-lines, to fit these words.
        Write each syllable under the note or notes to which it is to be sung.

10

There were three men came out of the west
Their fortune for to try.   *Folksong, 'John Barleycorn'*

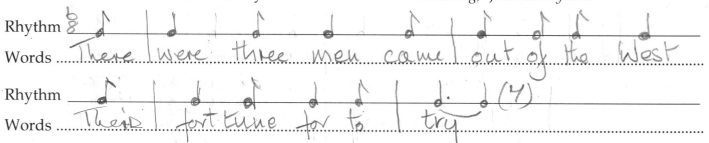

   OR
   (b) Write a four-bar rhythm in $\frac{6}{4}$ time. Include the following groups of notes in your rhythm:

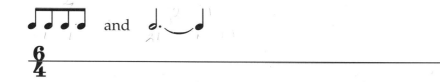

3 Name each of the following notes, as in the given example.

10

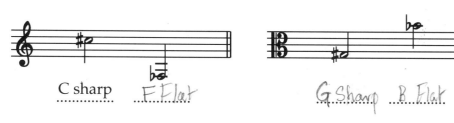

C sharp   F Flat   G Sharp B Flat   F double   G Sharp
                                                    Sharp.

4 Rewrite the following using the bass clef but keeping the pitch the same. 10

Holst, 'In the bleak midwinter'

5 Add the correct clefs and any necessary sharp or flat signs to make the scales named below. Do not use key signatures. 10

G♯ minor melodic

A♭ major

6 (a) Write a chromatic scale in crotchets (quarter notes), beginning and ending on the given notes. Take notice of the key signature, and do not use unnecessary accidentals. 10

(b) Describe fully each of the following intervals.

Interval ....diminished 4ᵗ..........

..........minor 6ᵗʰ..........

7 (a) Name each of the numbered chords as tonic, subdominant or dominant. The key is G major. 10

Carol, 'Es ist ein' Ros' entsprungen'

(1) (2) (3)

Chord

1 ..subdominant..

2 ..Tonic..........

3 ..Dominant......

(b) Write the named triads without key signatures. Remember to add any necessary sharp or flat signs.

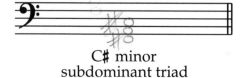

C♯ minor
subdominant triad

B♭ major
dominant triad

8 Here is part of the 1st violin part from Pomp and Circumstance March No.4 by Elgar.
Look at it and then answer the questions below.

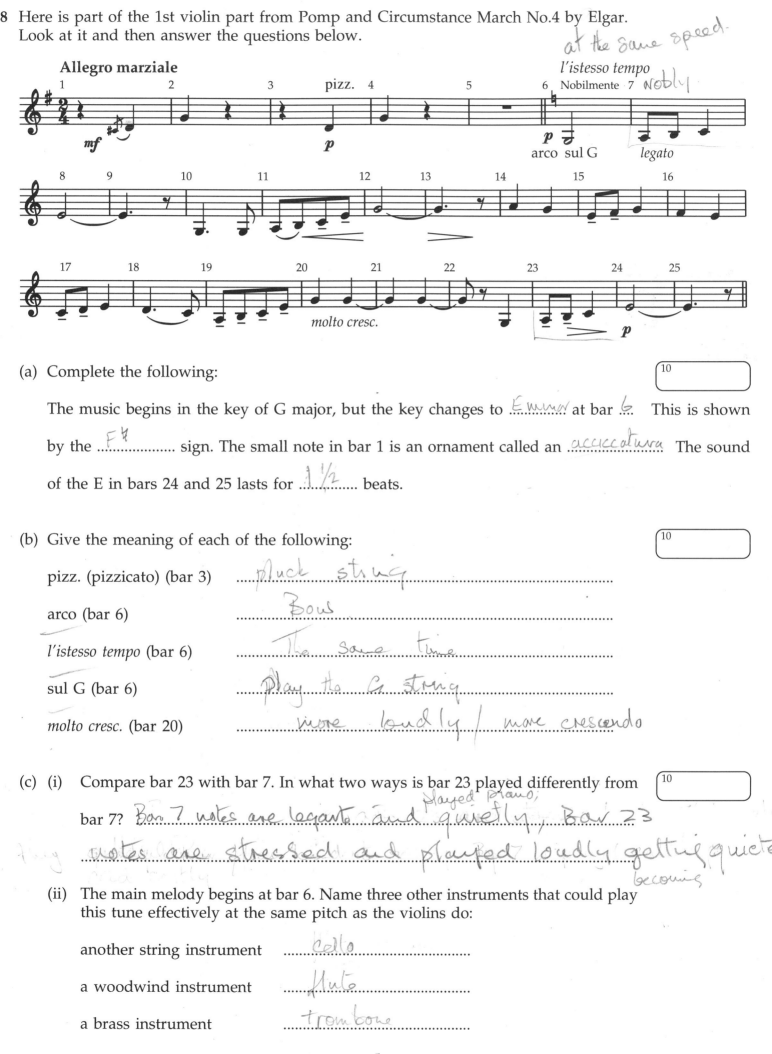

(a) Complete the following:

[10]

The music begins in the key of G major, but the key changes to *E minor* at bar *6*. This is shown

by the *F♯* sign. The small note in bar 1 is an ornament called an *acciccatura* The sound

of the E in bars 24 and 25 lasts for *1½* beats.

(b) Give the meaning of each of the following:

[10]

pizz. (pizzicato) (bar 3) ...... *pluck string* ......

arco (bar 6) ...... *Bow* ......

l'istesso tempo (bar 6) ...... *The same time* ......

sul G (bar 6) ...... *Play the G string* ......

molto cresc. (bar 20) ...... *more loudly / more crescendo* ......

(c) (i) Compare bar 23 with bar 7. In what two ways is bar 23 played differently from

[10]

bar 7? *Bar 7 notes are legarto and played piano; quietly, Bar 23*
notes are stressed and played loudly getting quieter becoming

(ii) The main melody begins at bar 6. Name three other instruments that could play
this tune effectively at the same pitch as the violins do:

another string instrument ...... *cello* ......

a woodwind instrument ...... *flute* ......

a brass instrument ...... *trombone* ......

5

Theory Paper Grade 4   1995   B

Duration 2 hours

Candidates should answer ALL questions.
Write your answers on this paper — no others will be accepted.
Answers must be written clearly and neatly — otherwise marks may be lost.

1 (a) Add the missing bar-lines to the following. Also add a rest or rests at the place
   marked * to complete the bar.

Chopin, Ballade, Op.23

(b) Add the time signature to the following, and add a single rest at each place marked *.

Brahms, *Requiem*

2 **EITHER**
  (a) Write a rhythm on one note, with time signature and bar-lines, to fit these words.
      Write each syllable under the note or notes to which it is to be sung.

      'O father, O father, build me a boat
      That over the ocean I may float.'   *Anon.*

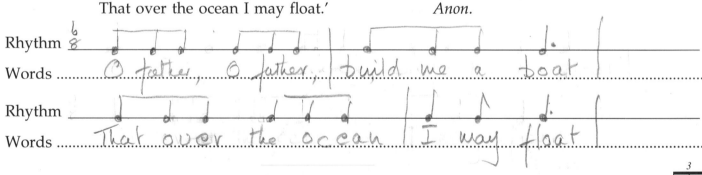

  OR
  (b) Write a four-bar rhythm in ⁴⁄₈ time. Include the following group of notes in your rhythm:
      and also include a semiquaver (16th note) rest.

3 Name each of the following notes, as in the given example.

C flat   A sharp   B double flat   F flat   C double   A natural
                                                   sharp

4 Rewrite the following using the alto clef but keeping the pitch the same.

Elgar, Introduction and Allegro for Strings

5 Write the scales named below, using the given rhythm.

10

F♯ minor harmonic, descending, without key signature but adding any necessary sharp or flat signs

D♭ major, ascending, with key signature

6 Write the following intervals, using notes from the scale of F harmonic minor.
Write the key signature for each example.

10

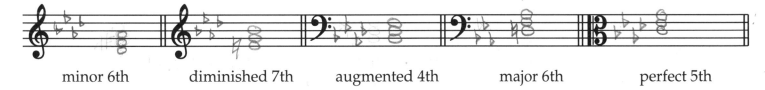

minor 6th   diminished 7th   augmented 4th   major 6th   perfect 5th

7 (a) Name each of the numbered chords as tonic, subdominant or dominant.
The key is B♭ major.

10

Gauntlett

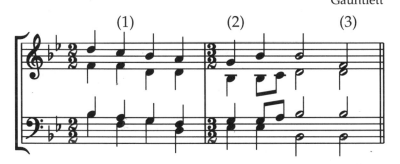

Chord

1 Dominant

2 Subdominant

3 Tonic

(b) Write the named triads, as shown by the key signatures.

major key
subdominant triad

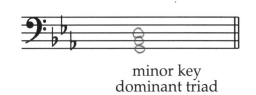

minor key
dominant triad

8 Here is part of the melody from Air for bassoon and piano, by Christopher Brown.
Look at it and then answer the questions below.

(a) Give the meaning of each of the following: [10]

⌣ (bar 1) ......Legarto...

⌢ (bar 2) ......slur or tie...

rit. (bar 7) ......hold back..

a tempo (bar 8) ......return to tempo...

legato (bar 8) ......play the notes smothly...

(b) (i) Over the stave in bar 1, the beats of the bar have been printed at the correct places. Write the beats in the same way over bars 2 and 3. [10]

(ii) Here is bar 5 written out in ¾ time, but so that it sounds the same.
Rewrite bars 6 and 7 in the same way.

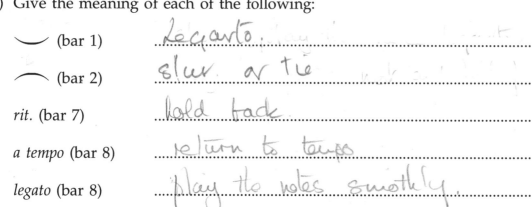

(c) (i) The bassoon is a woodwind instrument. Name two other instruments that could effectively play this melody at the same pitch: [10]

a string instrument ...cello...   a brass instrument ...horn...

(ii) Although there is no key signature, bars 3–6 are in the key of C minor. Give the technical names in C minor (tonic, supertonic, etc.) of:

the note in bar 4 ...dominant...   the first note in bar 5 ...mediant...

(iii) Write the first note in bar 5 in the treble clef so that it sounds at the same pitch, but with the time value of a breve (double whole note).

Theory Paper Grade 4   1995   C

Duration 2 hours

Candidates should answer ALL questions.
Write your answers on this paper — no others will be accepted.
Answers must be written clearly and neatly — otherwise marks may be lost.

1 (a) Rewrite the following from bar 2, grouping the notes correctly. Also add a rest to
complete the last bar in your version.

[10]

Bizet, *Carmen*

(b) Rewrite bar 3 using notes of *double the length,* and complete the new time signature.

2 **EITHER**
(a) Write a rhythm on one note, with time signature and bar-lines, to fit these words.
Write each syllable under the note or notes to which it is to be sung.

[10]

Johnny Morgan played on the organ,
Jimmy played on the drum.   *Playground rhyme*

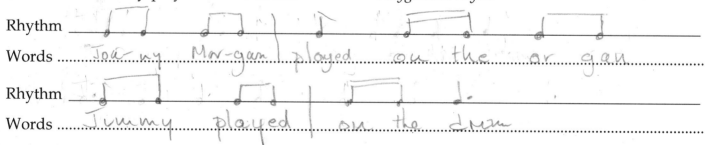

OR
(b) Write a four-bar rhythm in $\frac{9}{8}$ time. Include the following groups of notes in your rhythm:

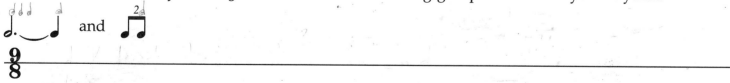

3 Name each of the following notes, as in the given example.

[10]

E flat   C Sharp   B double flat   F double sharp   C flat   D natural

9

4 Rewrite the following using the alto clef but keeping the pitch the same.

'Eriskay love lilt'

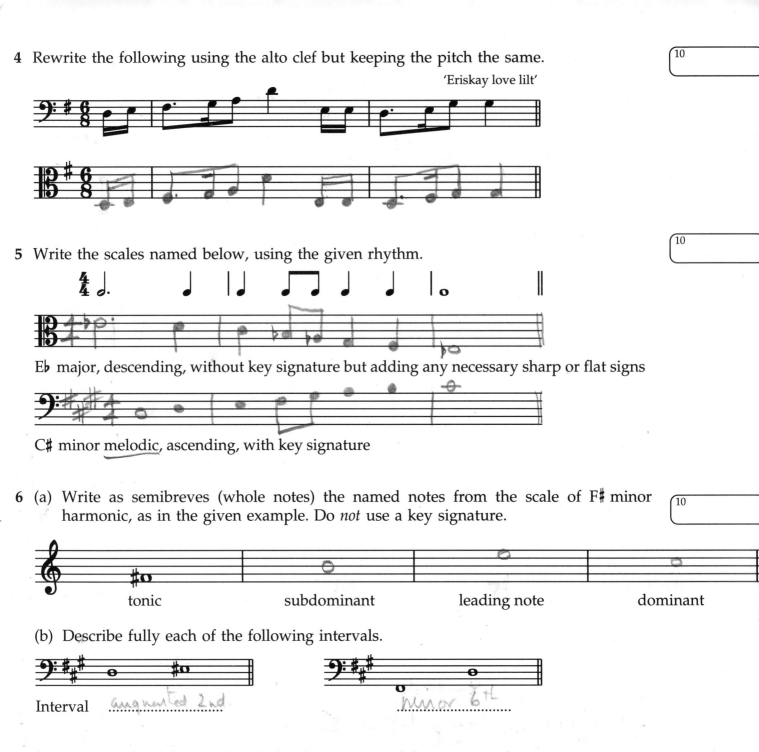

5 Write the scales named below, using the given rhythm.

Eb major, descending, without key signature but adding any necessary sharp or flat signs

C# minor melodic, ascending, with key signature

6 (a) Write as semibreves (whole notes) the named notes from the scale of F# minor harmonic, as in the given example. Do *not* use a key signature.

tonic   subdominant   leading note   dominant

(b) Describe fully each of the following intervals.

Interval   Augmented 2nd   minor 6th

7 (a) Name each of the numbered chords as tonic, subdominant or dominant.
The key is Bb major.

Stanford, 'The Old Superb'

(1)   (2)   (3)

B F D   F A

Chord

1 .....Mediant.....

2 .....Dominant.....

3 .....sub dom in ant.....

(b) Write the key signature and the named triad in B minor.

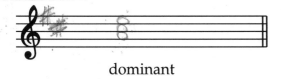

dominant

10

8 Here is the melody line from a part of Chopin's Mazurka, Op.7 No.1, for piano. Look at it and then answer the questions below.

(a) (i) Name the key of the music in bars 1 to 4. ....

[10]

(ii) Give the number of a bar in which the notes and timing are the same as bar 17. Bar ...19...

(iii) From the double bar in bar 12 the music changes key. Name the new key. *G minor*

(iv) Explain ⌐⌐⌐ (3) in bar 20. ...play the 3 quavers in time of one crotchet...

(v) What is the name of the ornament in bar 4? ...trill...

(b) (i) Give the meaning of each of the following:

[10]

Vivace *quick & lively* ....quicker + lively...............

legato (bar 13) ....smoothly...............

poco rall. (bar 20) ....play a little slower............... *little slow*

(ii) Give the number of a bar in which an upper mordent appears. Bar ...8...

(iii) Write an enharmonic equivalent of the highest note of bar 11.

(c) (i) A Mazurka is a Polish dance. Look again at this example and describe the time this dance is in as: simple or compound; duple, triple or quadruple.

[10]

...Simple... ...triple...

(ii) Underline any of the following instruments which could play bars 1–4:

trombone   flute   violin   timpani   clarinet
                      p

(iii) Write on one line the rhythmic figure which can be found in each of the first twelve bars.

3/4   ...♪ semiquaver rest.

11

Theory Paper Grade 4   1995   S

Duration 2 hours

Candidates should answer ALL questions.
Write your answers on this paper — no others will be accepted.
Answers must be written clearly and neatly — otherwise marks may be lost.

TOTAL MARKS
100

1 (a) Complete the time signature at each place marked * in the following.

Brahms, Romanze, Op.118 No.5

(b) Rewrite the following in notes of *half the value*, and add the new time signature.
Also describe the time (simple or compound; duple, triple or quadruple).

Delius, *Sea Drift*

Time *Compound Time*

2 EITHER

(a) Write a rhythm on one note, with time signature and bar-lines, to fit these words.
Write each syllable under the note or notes to which it is to be sung.

> Beasts did leap and birds did sing,
> Trees did grow and plants did spring.   *Richard Barnfield*

Rhythm

Words ...... Beast, did leap and birds did sing

Rhythm

Words ...... Trees, did grow, and plants, did spring

OR

(b) Write a four-bar rhythm in $\frac{2}{2}$ time. Include the following note and group of notes in your rhythm:

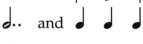

$\frac{2}{2}$

3 Name each of the following notes, as in the given example.

10

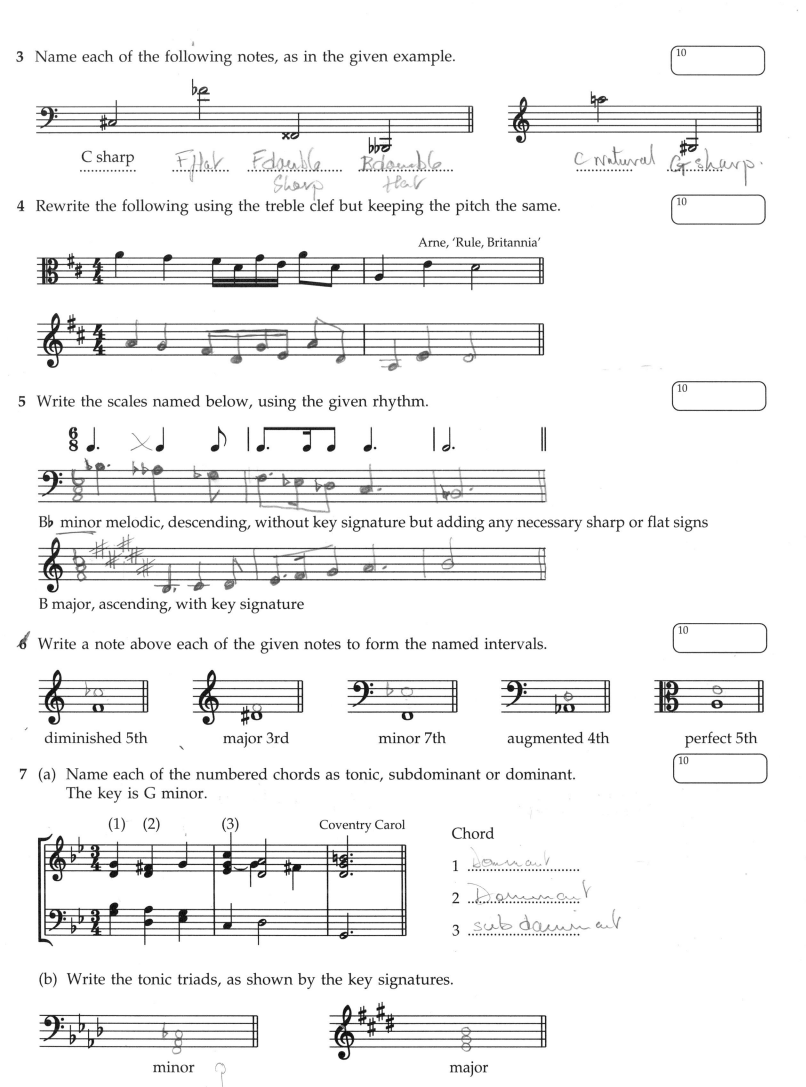

C sharp   F flat   F double   B double
                          Sharp   Flat

C natural   G sharp.

4 Rewrite the following using the treble clef but keeping the pitch the same.

10

Arne, 'Rule, Britannia'

5 Write the scales named below, using the given rhythm.

10

Bb minor melodic, descending, without key signature but adding any necessary sharp or flat signs

B major, ascending, with key signature

6 Write a note above each of the given notes to form the named intervals.

10

diminished 5th   major 3rd   minor 7th   augmented 4th   perfect 5th

7 (a) Name each of the numbered chords as tonic, subdominant or dominant.
The key is G minor.

10

(1)   (2)   (3)   Coventry Carol

Chord

1 Dominant

2 Dominant

3 sub dominant

(b) Write the tonic triads, as shown by the key signatures.

minor   major

13

8 This theme is taken from the *Academic Festival Overture* by Brahms.
Look at it and then answer the questions below.

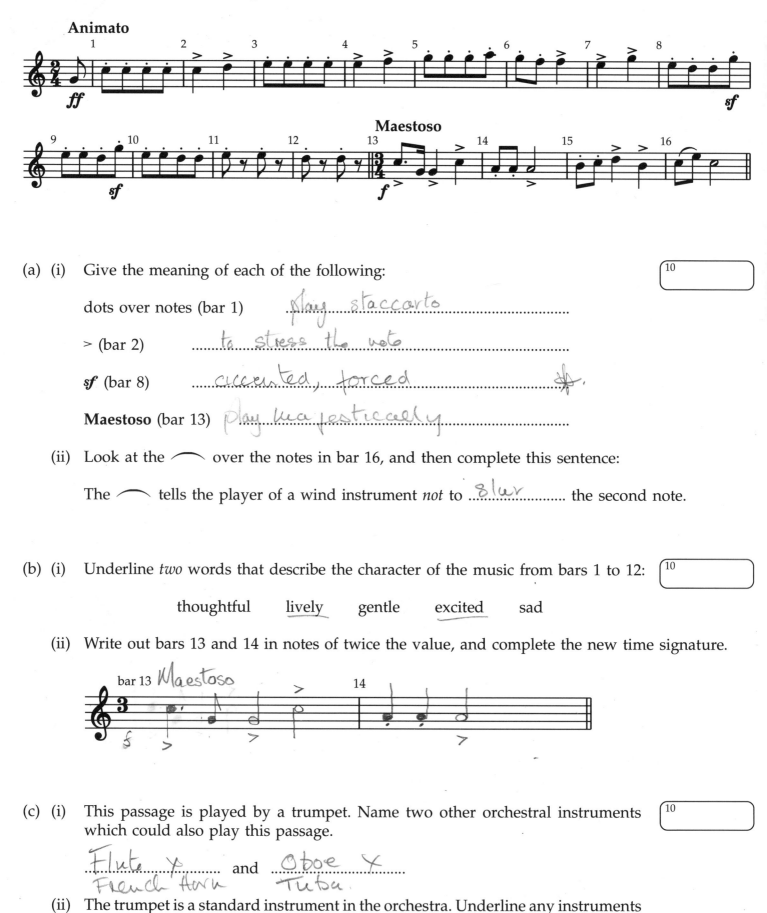

(a) (i) Give the meaning of each of the following:

dots over notes (bar 1) ......Play staccarto.....................

> (bar 2) ....to stress the note................

sf (bar 8) ....accented, forced.........................

Maestoso (bar 13) Play majestically...........................

(ii) Look at the ⌒ over the notes in bar 16, and then complete this sentence:

The ⌒ tells the player of a wind instrument *not* to ....slur........... the second note.

(b) (i) Underline *two* words that describe the character of the music from bars 1 to 12:

thoughtful   <u>lively</u>   gentle   <u>excited</u>   sad

(ii) Write out bars 13 and 14 in notes of twice the value, and complete the new time signature.

(c) (i) This passage is played by a trumpet. Name two other orchestral instruments which could also play this passage.

....Flute x...... and ....Oboe x......
French Horn   Tuba.

(ii) The trumpet is a standard instrument in the orchestra. Underline any instruments in this list which are *not* standard members of the orchestra:

double bass   <u>guitar</u>   <u>recorder</u>   oboe   organ   timpani